The Sacrament of Holy Communion

by Patti Thisted Arthur

THE SACRAMENT OF HOLY COMMUNION

Copyright © 1999 by
CSS Publishing Company, Inc.
Lima, Ohio

ISBN 0-7880-1351-3

Holy Communion is a sacrament.
Lutheran Christians believe that
there are two sacraments:
Holy Baptism and Holy Communion.

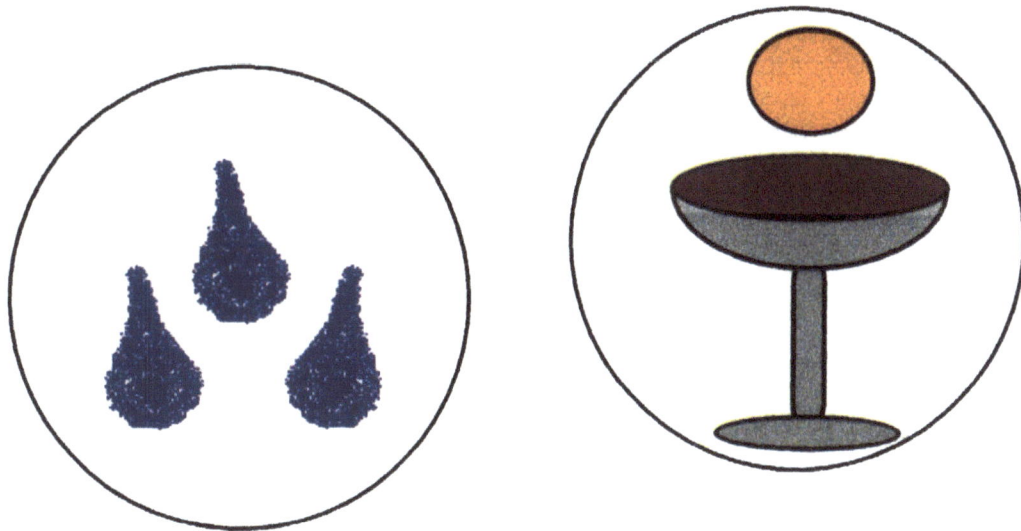

Both of these sacraments are gifts
from God.
We cannot earn them.
We cannot buy them.
Sacraments are ways that we can
see, feel, hear, smell, and taste
God's love and forgiveness.

A sacrament is something that...

Jesus told us to do,

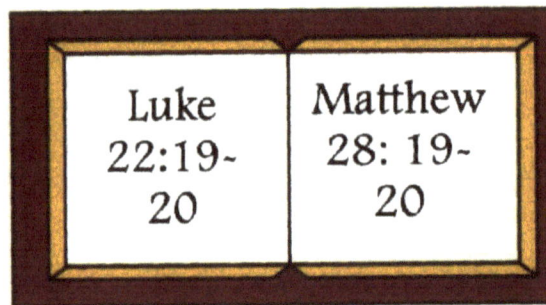

Luke 22:19-20	Matthew 28: 19-20

and uses something from the earth,

and brings us God's grace and forgiveness.

During Communion, Christians gather together and eat a bit of bread and drink a sip of wine that has been consecrated by a pastor. It is when the bread and wine are consecrated that Jesus becomes part of those elements. Communion is a special meal that God has given to us because God loves us.

Communion is usually given at the altar.
Sometimes we call Holy Communion other names,
such as the Lord's Supper or the Communion
meal, because we eat bread and drink wine that
is given to us by God as a very special gift.

The altar looks like a table, because it is where
we gather to eat this meal that God gives to us.

Christians gather at the altar in much the same
way that families gather at the table for meals
at home. We call all Christians together the
Christian family or the body of Christ because
God joins us all together with his love.

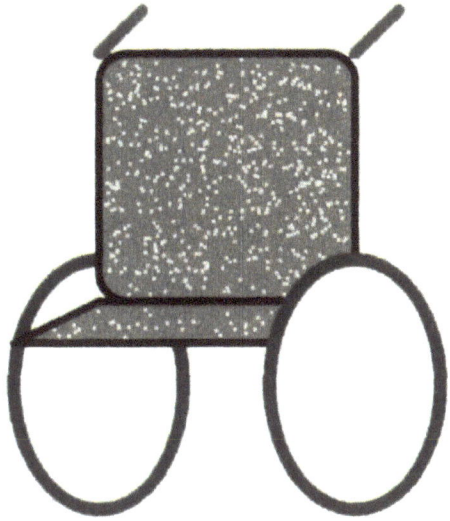

Some people cannot come to the altar, and so those people take Communion wherever they are: sitting in their pew, in their homes, or wherever they may be.

God loves us so much that he comes to us wherever we are. That is why Communion can be taken wherever a person is.

How did Communion start?

The first Communion meal was the last supper that Jesus had with his disciples. Jesus and his disciples were celebrating the Passover meal, which is a Jewish tradition celebrated every year.

This Passover meal was first shared by the Israelites on the night before Moses led the Israelites out of slavery in Egypt. In the story, written in Exodus 12, God told all of the Israelites to mark their door frames with the blood of a lamb. The angel of death would come, but would pass over all of those houses marked with blood. Instead, the angel of death went to the houses of the Egyptians to claim all of their firstborn. After God did this, the Pharaoh said that the Israelite slaves could leave Egypt.

God commanded that the Passover meal be celebrated every year on the anniversary of the exodus from Egypt.

While Jesus and the disciples were celebrating the Passover, Jesus began the sacrament of Holy Communion. The story of this Passover meal is written in Matthew 26, Mark 14, and Luke 22.

The words of Jesus that are written in the Bible are the same words that the pastor says as he or she consecrates the bread and wine for Holy Communion.

Jesus commanded that Holy Communion be celebrated to remember him and for the forgiveness of sins.

We take Holy Communion because we want to

...do what Jesus told us to do.

...remember and celebrate how much God loves us.

...receive forgiveness for our sins.

...grow in faith.

...celebrate and worship the wonderful gifts of God, especially the gift of Jesus.

...strengthen our relationship with God.

...be joined with all of the other saints in the Body of Christ.

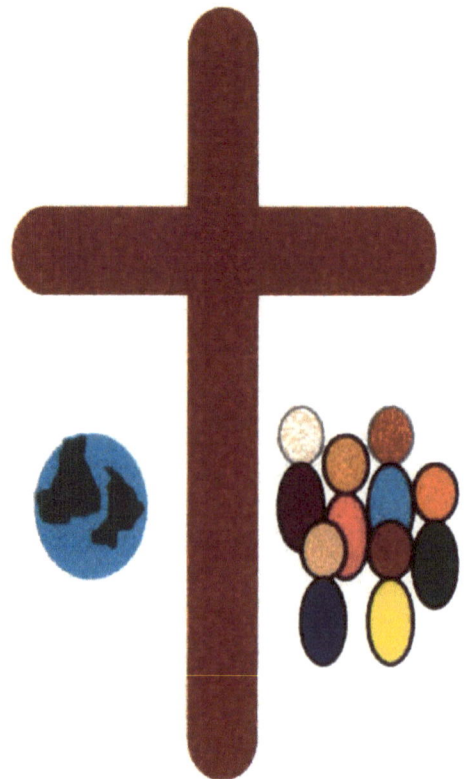

How does all of this happen?

There are two elements that are used in Communion: bread and wine.

Bread and wine were what Jesus used when Communion was first distributed at the Passover meal with the disciples.

Today, we still use bread and wine.

There are several different ways that the Communion elements can be shared.

Unleavened (made without yeast) wafers are often used, following the tradition of unleavened bread used at the Passover. Many congregations use loaves of bread, breaking off a piece for each communicant. The wafer or small piece of bread may be placed in the mouth or in the hand of each communicant.

Wine is placed in either a large cup or in individual cups. Communicants may either drink from the large cup or drink from individual cups. If intinction is used, the pastor or communion assistant will dip the wafer into the wine and give it to the communicant.

We believe that Jesus is present in the bread and the wine during Communion.

We cannot explain exactly how Jesus is present in the bread and the wine. We call it a mystery because only God knows the answer.

Throughout Communion, the bread remains bread, and the wine remains wine.

However, we believe Jesus Christ becomes present in, with, and under these things from earth, because Jesus said, " This is my body and this is my blood, given for you for the forgiveness of sins."

Many different items are used during Holy Communion. Each of those things has a name.

Pall - a stiff, white square used to cover the chalice.

Paten - the plate that holds the bread for Holy Communion.

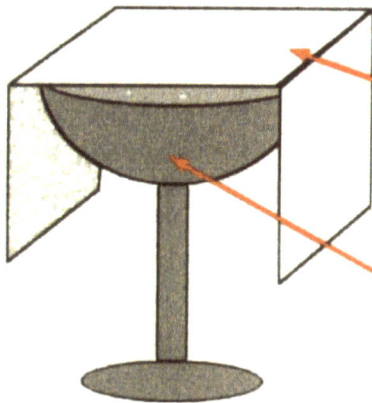

Purificator - a square linen napkin used to clean the rim of the chalice during Holy Communion.

Chalice - the cup that holds the wine for Holy Communion.

Flagon - the storage container from which wine is poured for Holy Communion.

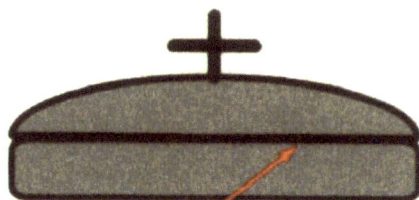

Ciborium - a container with a lid that stores bread for Holy Communion.

Veil - a cloth placed over all of these items before and after Holy Communion. In some congregations, this cloth is the color of the current church season.

Things To Think About

~ What does Communion mean to me?

~ Why do we make such a big deal about Communion?

~ How often should we have Communion?

~ How does Communion join me together with all Christians everywhere?

~ Questions that I have:

Words to know

Chalice - the cup that holds the wine for Holy Communion.

Ciborium - a container with a lid that stores bread for Holy Communion.

communicant - a person who receives Holy Communion.

communion assistant - a person who helps the pastor distribute Holy Communion.

consecrate - to set apart as holy for religious use.

elements - the items from the earth used in the sacraments - water for Holy Baptism and bread and wine for Holy Communion.

Flagon - the storage container from which wine is poured for Holy Communion.

forgiveness - to wipe away a sin, as if it never existed.

grace - God's love and forgiveness, given freely to God's children.

intinction - distribution of Holy Communion by dipping the wafer into the wine.

Pall - a stiff, white square used to cover the chalice for Holy Communion.

Paten - the plate that holds the bread for Holy Communion.

Passover - the holiday that celebrates the escape of the Israelites from Egypt.

Purificator - a square linen napkin used to clean the rim of the chalice during Holy Communion.

sacrament - a rite commanded by Christ which uses an earthly element as a sign of God's grace. The two sacraments are Holy Baptism and Holy Communion.

sins - those things that are contrary to God's will that a person does, or those things that are God's will that a person does not do.

Veil - a cloth placed over all of the items used in Holy Communion before and after the celebration of the sacrament.

wafer - a thin piece of bread made without yeast.

www.ingramcontent.com/pod-product-compliance
Lightning Source LLC
Chambersburg PA
CBHW041224040426
42443CB00002B/85